Acknowledgements

To all who have supported me over the years, thank you.
Glory to God, for He is faithful!

Pearls of Wisdom from Psalms 1 to 10

By Pauline Russ

PSALM ONE

BLESSED IS THE MAN

Blessed is the man that does not keep company with ungodly people or sinners or sit with scornful people. His passion should be to study and mediate on God's word day and night. If he does the above he shall be blessed and overly filled with blessings just like the trees by the river. They will receive plenty of water for growth and will not wither.

Sinners will not receive the blessings. They are like dried up grass that the wind blows away. So the ungodly or sinners will not stand among the righteous in the judgement. God knows who is righteous and the ways of the ungodly people will be punished.

Notes:

PSALM TWO

THOU ART MY SON

Why do earthly people rage and plan evil plots?
The king and rulers meet to fight and plot against
the Lord's Holy words. They say let us break the
chains and throw away the ropes from us. God
will sit in the heavens and laugh mocking them.
The Lord warns them and frightens them with his
angry. The Lord said I have selected my own king
and he will rule Jerusalem from my holy
mountain.

The lord will declare that this is my son and I am
his father. I will give you the nations if you ask and
all the earthly people will be yours. You will
punish them with an iron rod if they disobey you
and break them into pieces like a clay pot.

Rulers be wise and learn this lesson. Serve the
lord with fear but be joyful. Show God that you
are loyal to his son or you will perish. Happy are
the people that trust the son for protection.

Notes:

PSALM THREE

I WILL NOT BE AFRAID

Lord how many enemies do I have? Many of them revolted against me. Many say that God will not rescue me. But God, you are a hedge of protection around me. Your glory shines on me. I will not be afraid. I cry out to you lord and you answer me from the heavens.

I go to bed and sleep. I wake up because the Lord protects me. I will not be afraid of my enemies. Even if ten thousand are at my sides. Arise o Lord and save me. Fight of my enemies and stop the wicked in their plots. From the Lord comes protection and safety. His blessing is on his people.

Notes:

PSALM FOUR

HEAR ME WHEN I CALL

Answer my calls oh Heavenly Father. Give me peace in my storms. Have compassion and mercy please hear my prayer. How long will my children turn my glory into shame and disgrace? How long will you love false beliefs and worship idols.

Know that there is only one true God our Lord. And God will hear me when I call to him. It's alright to get angry but do not sin. When lying in your bed at night. Be silent search your heart and meditate on the lord. Offer up praise and trust in God.

Lord let people see your light in your children. Nothing can out do the joy that you give me Lord. I can lay down in peace knowing that my God watches over me.

Notes:

PSALM FIVE

IN THE MORNING

Oh Lord, please listen closely to my words and my sadness. Hear me when I cry out for help. My savior and God I pray only to you. In the morning, you hear my call and I pray to you my request and desires and wait patiently for your response. You are a God who does not tolerate evil or wickedness.

The proud and arrogant is not welcome in your presence. You hate all wrong doers and destroy liars, deceitfulness and murders men. I by your great mercy will come into your house of worship with reverence and bow down towards your holy temple.

Order my steps in your righteousness because of my enemies. Show me your way Lord. Nothing said by the enemy can be trusted and their heart is filled with wickedness. Their deceitful words are leading them to their open grave. Find them guilty, Lord. Let their underhanded plotting be their downfall.

Exile them for their many sins for they have resisted your godly authority. Let your children who depend on your loving protection to be glad and joyful in songs. Spread your holy covering over them that love you and may praise your holy name.

O God you bless the faithful children of God. You surround them with your glory and favor.

Notes:

PSALM SIX

THE LORD HAS HEARD

O Lord please do not scold or punish me while angry or mad at me. Show me compassion Lord because I am weak. Please heal me Lord because my body rack with pain. How much longer will my soul be in pain. Don't leave O Lord; save me because of your unconditional love.

Everyone forgets about you when you're dead. No one can praise you from the grave. I am worn out from stress and pain. I cry all night until by bed linen is wet and my couch damp from my tears. My eyes grow weak with sadness because of all of my enemies. All evil doers stay away from me because the lord has heard my cry for mercy.

The Lord has answered my prayers and my enemies are embarrassed and upset. They will turn away in shame because their weapons did not prosper.

Notes:

Psalm Seven

In Thee Do I Put My Trust

O Lord you are my armor of protection. Save me from my enemies who pursue me or they will tear me a part like a lion. Lord have I done wrong? Have I done wrong to my fellow man? Have I stolen from enemies? If I am guilty let my enemies capture me and hold me hostage. Let them trample me into the ground until I am buried.

O Lord come against my raging enemies with your wrath and demand fairness. Call together all nations and rule your people from above. Judge the people and defend me. Show that I am right and have done no wrong.

 Lord you know our thoughts and feelings. Put a stop to the actions of the wicked people and help the righteous. God please protect us under your wings and save these with a good heart. God is a just God he judges by what is right. He is prepared to punish the wicked when they refuse to change their ways. God will prepare his bow to use against evil people.

Anyone who is absorbed with evil is full of trouble. They are disillusion about their end and are digging their graves. I will praise and thank the Lord for his righteousness. I will sing glory unto his name, the Almighty God.

Notes:

Psalm Eight

How Excellent is Thy Name

Oh Lord, our God how splendor is your name in the entire world. You have set our heavenly bliss above the heavens. The lips of children and infants have been anointed to praise you because of your enemies and to silence the enemy and avenger.

When I look up into the sky and think about your works with your fingers that created the moon and stars to sit in the sky. What is man that you love him so much you made him a little lower than angels in heaven and crown him with great adoration and honor? You put him a ruler in charge of works by your hand and over all creatures of the earth. Oh lord, our God how splendor is your name in the entire world.

Notes:

Psalm Nine

With My Whole Heart

I will praise you Lord with all my heart, mind, and soul. I will tell everyone of all the great things you have done. You make me happy and full of joy oh God I will sing praises unto you. My enemies turn away frustrated and die before you. You have listened to my complaints you judge fairly as you sit on your throne.

You scold all the different nations and destroy the wicked people wiping their name completely from remembrance. The enemy will never ever come back again. God has destroyed their cities and they will not be remembered. But our God will always rule. Sitting on his throne God will Judge.

He will judge the word righteously. He will judge fairly. The Lord protects the helpless. He protects them in troubled times. His people trust him. God will not abandon his children. Sing praises unto God who sits high in the heavens. Tell everyone about what God has done. He remembers who has murdered and those who have suffered. Lord helps me see how my enemies hurt me. Do not let me die.

I will praise you because you will save me. The nations have falling into their own pits. They are caught in their own nets. Everyone knows that God makes just decisions. The wicked set themselves up to fall into their own traps. Wicked people will die also those who forget God.

The poor will not be forgotten. God will remember their hopes. God is going to rise up to judge man. They will not triumph over God. God teach the nation to fear you and show you reverence. They are human but you're God.

Notes:

Psalm Ten

Thou Has Seen Thou Has Heard

Lord there is trouble and I feel all alone. I feel that you are not with me; the wicked proudly hunt the helpless. They plot to catch them. They brag and boast about the things they want. They bless the wicked and the greedy but despise the Lord. The wicked are so proud that they do not search for God or even think about him.

The wicked always seem to prosper. They are sneaky, and your commandments mean nothing to him. They even torment their enemies. They think they are invincible and that nothing can happen to them. I will never be shamed. Their tongues are full of swearing, lies, and deceit. They use their tongues to speak evil and sin.

They hid near people's homes and laid in wait to kill innocent people. They hide and watch their prey in secret. They trap the poor in nets. The poor are thrown down and crushed, too weak to defeat the wicked. They think God don't see them and has forgotten about them. God make your needs known and will punish the wicked. Don't forget the helpless that need you, oh Lord!.

Why do evil people hate God? They think God will not punish them. Lord I know you see these cruel and evil things. Lord do something about these wicked and evil people. Your People look up to you when in trouble. You're the one that helps the poor. Put an end to the power of wicked men. Punish them for their evil ways.

Lord God is king forever and ever. Take your land back from the nations who refuse to worship you. Lord you have heard the prayers of your people. Listen to them and answer them as they pray. Protect the poor and put an end to their suffering. Then, they will no longer be afraid of evil and wicked people.

Notes:

www.ingramcontent.com/pod-product-compliance
Lightning Source LLC
Chambersburg PA
CBHW040347060426
42445CB00029B/33